POTTY POLITICS

Potty politics

Deary, terry

D1333993

Linw

To Stan Jinks
with thanks for the additional research

POTTY POLITICS

TERRY DEARY

LINWOOD HIGH SCHOOL LIBRARY

Illustrated by
Tony Reeve

Hippo

103023

(320)
.94.)

Scholastic Children's Books,
Commonwealth House, 1–19 New Oxford Street,
London WC1A 1NU, UK
A division of Scholastic Limited
London ~ New York ~ Toronto ~ Sydney ~ Auckland

Published by Scholastic Limited, 1996

Text copyright © Terry Deary 1996
Illustrations copyright © Tony Reeve 1996

All rights reserved

ISBN 0 439 01380 1

Typeset by TW Typesetting, Midsomer Norton, Avon
Printed and bound by Nørhaven Paperback, Viborg, Denmark

6 8 10 9 7 5

The right of Terry Deary and Tony Reeve to be identified as the author and
illustrator of this work respectively has been asserted by them in accordance with
the Copyright, Designs and Patents Act, 1988.

This book is sold subject to the condition that it shall not, by way of trade or
otherwise be lent, resold, hired out, or otherwise circulated without the publisher's
prior consent in any form of binding other than that in which it is published and
without a similar condition, including this condition, being imposed upon the
subsequent purchaser.

Contents

Terry Deary wanted to be a Member of Parliament when he was five years old. Sadly they don't have five-year-old MPs. . . just grown-ups who act that way. Anyway, he wouldn't have been a very good MP because he's too clever, too honest and too good

looking. . . he says. When Terry failed to win the Mr Universe title, he took up writing books instead because it doesn't need so many muscles. He lives and works in his County Durham home where he has written over 70 books for boys, girls, gorillas – anyone who'll read him in fact.

Tony Reeve *never* wanted to be a politician – they're too potty. He much prefers making fun of them in his cartoons. In fact, there's so much to make fun of that he's been doing this for over ten years and he's still very busy! He's worked on parent-friendly papers and

mags like the *Independent* and *Private Eye*, and he lives in London where he can keep a close eye on the potty goings on at Westminster!

INTRODUCTION

Politics is Potty. When you're a child your parents tell you what to do. When you go to school then your teachers tell you what to do. And when you grow up Members of Parliament (also called MPs) pass laws and tell you what to do. But people actually *vote* for these Members of Parliament! Potty!

Members of Parliament who will take your money off you (and call it "tax"). That's like voting for your parents to cut your pocket money...

Members of Parliament will tell you what you can or can't do! It's like voting for teachers to punish you...

You vote for Members of Parliament to run your life for you.

That's potty politics for you. And if you don't want to grow up as a potty political person then you should know all about it.

In the words of the old saying, "If you can't beat them, join them." Learn how to become a politician. and start here.

WHO WANTS TO BE A POLITICIAN?

Quick quote: "A good politician is as unlikely as an honest burglar." (Menken)

Do you ever get bored? Bored with the thought of maths on a Monday morning? Or mother moaning about dad's dirty socks?

Why not get away from it all?

Become a politician!

Stand for election and become your local MP!

This is not a problem!

Simply lie about your age.[1]

This will be good practice for when you become a politician. Several Politicians have, throughout history been caught out telling little fibs ... and some have been caught telling whacking great porkie pie *lies*! It's all part of the game.

---

[1] Of course the problem is that you may be found out ... some spoil-sport teacher may recognize you and give the game away. In that case you would *not* be allowed to take your place in Parliament. You could try disguising yourself with a beard, but a survey in 1996 said that beards were not popular with voters. MPs were advised to shave them off – especially the women.

Top tips 1: Telling lies

When you get into Parliament you will have to follow new rules. One of these rules says you cannot call another Member of Parliament a "liar". So, if you catch someone "lying" you may say:

"You have uttered a terminological inexactitude." (Winston Churchill said that. Never mind what it means, just learn it and impress your friends!)

"You are misleading the House." (The House of Commons, that is.)

"You are deceiving the House."

"You are being badly advised." (So you'd be advised to tell the truth from now on.)

"You are being economical with the truth."

Potty political fact: Naughty names

"Liar" is not the only naughty word. You can also call other Members of Parliament the following words which have all been used in the past ...

...but the trouble is you will be thrown out of Parliament.

If you want to insult another MP (but *not* be thrown out) then you ARE allowed to call them ...

Of course Americans do everything bigger and better than the Brits ... so their politicians are bigger and better liars. President George Bush is not remembered for much, but he is remembered for saying, "Watch my lips. There will be no new taxes." What happened next? He increased taxes, of course.

And George Washington, the first American President, is a wonderful example. Have you ever heard the story of young George Washington's father finding his cherry tree cut down? "Who did this?" he demanded.

Little George answered, "I can't tell a lie, Pa; you know I can't tell a lie. I did cut it with my hatchet!"

An honest politician? *No.* Because the whole story was made up by a writer called Weems. It is the biggest lie of all!

Foul fibbers

When British politicians fail to tell the truth it may be because they are a bit dim. When Neville Chamberlain came back from talking to Mr Hitler in 1938 he proudly declared, "Peace in our time." In 1939 he announced (less proudly), "This country is now at war with Germany."

British politicians are also quite good at avoiding questions. Ask a politician, "Are you going to knock down our house to build the new by-pass?" A cunning politician would answer, "It depends what you mean by the word 'by-pass'!"

By the time you've explained what you mean you have forgotten the question and he's off the hook.

If you want to be a Member of Parliament start practising now:

Top tips 2: How to avoid awkward questions

Some MPs can avoid questions by using their wits. In 1994 Labour MP Dennis Skinner asked a minister, "How many Government workers are a) men or b) women?" The minister replied immediately, "All of them!"

But if you are not that quick you need to practise *avoiding* questions.

Got the idea?
Then you are ready to become an MP.

I'm glad you asked me that! An extremely intelligent question which deserves an extremely intelligent answer! What do *you* think MP stands for?

What does the dictionary say?

Oh, I suppose I'll just have to tell you. An MP is a Member of Parliament. Someone elected by voters to represent them in the House of Commons.

CAN I BECOME ONE?

Are you over eighteen?

I think you will make an excellent MP.

Quick quote: The good news, if you want to be in politics, came in 1994 from late Labour leader John Smith. "I don't think brains are terribly important in politics." He said it!

Potty political glossary

Learn these words and phrases and become an instant expert on politics...

Another place Never mention those dreaded words, "the House of Commons", when you are in the House of Lords. Always call it "Another Place". And in the Commons you must talk about the House of Lords as the "Other Place". Don't ask why, just *do* it, even if it does seem potty.

Baker As in, "The children are having a *Baker Day* off school." In the 1980s the Minister for Education, Kenneth Baker, insisted that teachers have training days while children had a day off. They became known as "Baker Days". Some parents were shocked – they thought the children were having extra days off for *baking*! (Potty but true!)

CAP Once upon a time farmers raised animals and crops and sold them for cash. Then along came the European Community and its CAP … Common Agricultural Policy. The EC governments promised to buy anything the farmers didn't sell. Suddenly the governments found themselves with huge amounts of butter and beef that nobody wanted – they became known as the Beef Mountain and the Butter Mountain. These were joined by the Wine Lake! The CAP is politics at its pottiest.

Dawk A politician who is always arguing we should go to war is called a Hawk. Someone who is always saying we should make peace is called a Dove. Someone who can't make his mind up is called a Dawk. Simple when you think about it. Not to be confused with someone stupid enough to believe everything a politician says. They are known as a Dork.

Economical Someone who is economical doesn't use much. British Cabinet Secretary Sir Robert Armstrong didn't use much in the way of "truth" when he lied to an Australian court to protect the Conservative government from a scandal about spies. Of course in British politics no one is a "liar". Sir Robert simply confessed to being "economical with the truth". Unfortunately the Government were economical with the sack and he kept his job. Lying is *bad* – lying for Britain is *good*! Potty.

Falklands factor You are an unpopular Prime Minister and you are about to lose the next election. What do you do? Start a war! Because, in times of war, the whole country comes together and supports the government. In 1982 Mrs Thatcher, Conservative Prime Minister, was as popular as a slice of Christmas turkey on a vegetarian's plate until ... Argentina invaded some frozen rocks in the south Atlantic. *But* they were *British* rocks. Mrs Thatcher's Government declared war, won the war and went on to win the next election in 1983 ... even though some of their voters died defending the frozen rocks. Potty.

Gallup poll Some people can't wait for the election results to appear so they try to guess the result before it happens, usually before people have even voted. This is no different from guessing which horse will win a race before the race has started – that's more of a gallop poll, though. How can you guess the result of an election? Ask people which way they are going to vote, of course. You can't ask *all* the people so you ask a few and multiply the answer. In 1945, for example, 1,809 of the 25 million voters were asked and the poll got the result dead right. In 1992 the polls showed that Neil Kinnock's Labour Party would beat John Major's Conservatives. Er ... dead wrong. They had to hold Gallup polls to find out why the Gallup polls were wrong!

Hunger march In the 1930s many people were out of work and starving. One group decided to march down to London and ask the Government to help. The Jarrow Crusade was from a north-east town called, believe it or not, Jarrow. In Jarrow two out of three people were unemployed. The 200 marchers carried a petition with 11,572 signatures to Prime Minister Stanley Baldwin. They got a bishop's blessing and a lot of sympathy. What did Stan the Prime Man do? He refused to see them! So they all went home again ... on the train ... with very sore feet but no jobs.

I This is the name that most politicians call themselves. The monarch on the other hand often calls him or herself "We", as in " 'We' are not amused." This is known as the Royal "We" and is just a little potty. (Not to be confused with a Royal "Wee" which is aimed at an altogether different little potty.)

However, Mrs Thatcher became rather grand and royal towards the end of her 11-year spell as Prime Minister. People were astonished to hear her announce the birth of her granddaughter by saying:

Jeffrey Slang for £2,000. The amount of money (wrongly) said to have been paid by Conservative MP, Jeffrey Archer to a woman to stop her creating a scandal. Mr Archer sued the newspaper that said this and he won. But the slang word for £2,000 stuck.

Knock Knocking on doors is what politicians and their supporters have to do a lot if they want to get elected. However, some people would rather hide behind the sofa and pretend they are not in rather than talk to a politician. Others refuse to open the door. The best way around this is to use the following cunning plot...

Liberals In Queen Victoria's day the name of one of the two great political parties. Leader William

Gladstone went on so long he was known as the Grand Old Man. This was shortened to GOM. His Conservative enemy, Benjamin Disraeli, said it stood for God's Only Mistake. Cruel! In the 1920s the Liberals spent more time arguing amongst themselves than with the opposition and they fell apart. Now they are a very small party and it has been said they could save money by holding their Party Conference in a telephone box. This is a bit unfair since the British electoral system means they have very few MPs though they have lots of voters.

Mortal As in, "Is he mortal?" Prime Minister Robert Walpole used to ask this question about bishops in the House of Lords. What he meant was, "Can he be bribed?" Walpole certainly made a lot of money from crooked politics. He was even given a house as a gift. In fact he made so much money he could afford to give that house to Parliament for future Prime Ministers. It's a little terraced house called Number 10 Downing Street.

Nixon As in "It's a Nixon deal." American President Richard Nixon (affectionately called Tricky Dicky) was known for his dishonesty. A "Nixon" deal is a sly or illegal one – often to do with drugs. An ex-President said, "Nixon is a no-good liar. He can lie out of both sides of his mouth at the same time." Richard Nixon was about as dishonest as any number of politicians all over the world, but he broke the first rule of politics. Learn from your mistakes! Bribe, cheat or lie but (Rule 1), "Don't get caught!!" Nixon was caught lying and had to resign.

On yer bike This phrase usually means "Get lost," but in Parliament the politicians think of 1980s'

Conservative Norman Tebbitt. When unemployed people complained about the lack of work, tough, bald Norman – popularly known as the Chingford Skinhead – answered that his dad had been out of work so he'd got on his bike and ridden off to find some. The unemployed didn't like the suggestion that they were idle – they even twisted his words a bit and said Norman had told them, "Get on yer bike!" – or "Get lost!" You have to be very careful what you say ... even if you are a skinhead.

Pussy Ministers have little ministers to help them. They are called under-secretaries. A **P**arliamentary **U**nder **S**ecretary of **S**tate is known affectionately as a Pussy because of the initials. They are *not* allowed to have cat-naps in Parliament though. If they want to get promoted to being a minister they have to behave themselves. So, before they say something stupid, a Pussy will paws for thought and never be catty about ministers.

Queen's Speech Every September a new school year starts and the headteacher will probably drivel on about what s/he plans for the school in the next ten months. Parliament is like that. Its new year starts in October and the Queen drivels on about what "her" government will do in the next ten months. In fact her speech is written by the Prime Minister and so she just sits and reads out someone else's words. Why doesn't the Prime Minister just get up and say, "This is what *my* government is going to do?" Tradition. Potty.

Revolution Britain had a revolution long before the famous French Revolution. In 1649 Parliament voted (by a majority of just one) to chop off King Charles I's head. Then they had another (less bloody) revolution in 1688 to throw his son James II off the throne and invite William and Mary to take over – she was chopped-Charlie's granddaughter. There haven't been any serious threats of revolution since then, even though a party called the Communists said that it was the only way to get power for the people (see **Socialist** below). One of the most violent revolts was in 1381 when Wat Tyler's Peasants' Revolt killed tax collectors and lords before it was defeated. The peasants were fighting against a tax on everyone ... a Poll Tax. Unbelievably, Margaret Thatcher's Conservative Party introduced a Poll Tax in the 1980s. Riots followed again! Only potty politicians can repeat a dreadful mistake like that.

Socialist People who believe in giving power to the workers are often called Socialists. Their song is the *"Red Flag"* ... red because it is stained (they say) with the blood of the martyrs who died for the party. The gruesome words are sung to the jolly tune of

"Oh, Christmas Tree" and the first verse and chorus goes:

THE PEOPLE'S FLAG IS DEEPEST RED[2]
IT SHROUDED OFT OUR MARTYRED DEAD
AND ERE THEIR LIMBS GREW STIFF AND COLD
THEIR HEART'S BLOOD DYED ITS EVERY FOLD
SO RAISE THE SCARLET STANDARD HIGH
BENEATH ITS SHADE WE'LL LIVE AND DIE
THOUGH COWARDS FLINCH AND TRAITORS SNEER
WE'LL KEEP THE RED FLAG FLYING HERE

Now the Socialists are represented by the Labour Party. At a Party Conference in the 1980s the most hilarious sight was watching the leaders on the platform mouthing like goldfish because no one knew the words of the *"Red Flag"* song any more. The modern Labour politicians are about as "red" as a cucumber!

[2]But, if it was a *red* flag then the blood wouldn't show. How did they know that blood "dyed its every fold"? Unless, of course, the flag was in fact a *white* flag and the poor Socialist martyrs were waving it and trying to surrender! Maybe the song should be changed to "I do not really want to die / So keep that white flag flying high!"

Tory The nickname of the Conservative Party. If the Socialists are the party of the people then the Tories are the party of the posh and the ruling classes (kings, queens, dukes, traffic wardens and so on). The Tories are more often in power than the Socialists and there is a reason for this. If the Socialists do well and make the workers rich then the workers stop being workers and become posh. At the next election they all vote Tory and the Socialists are thrown out. In the 1990s the Socialists have at last found the answer to this problem ... they are making their party more posh than the Conservatives! Potty!

U-turn Politicians are experts at saying they will do one thing then suddenly going in the opposite direction – this is called a "U-turn" if you do it in a car. A popular 1950s play was called *"The Lady's not for Burning"* so Mrs Thatcher made a complicated joke out of this when people suggested she should do a U-turn in 1990. She said "You turn if you want ... but the Lady's not for turning." (You-turn ... U-turn, geddit?) While the party were still laughing at this brilliant witty word-play what did Mrs Thatcher do? A U-turn, of course!

Victory If you stick up two fingers at a teacher you will probably get some nasty punishment (like cleaning the graffiti off the girls' toilet walls). If you stick up two fingers at a policeman you will be arrested. But World War II Prime Minister Winston

V FOR VICTORY

Churchill stuck two fingers up at the whole nation

and got away with it! He had turned his hand around and said it was a "V for Victory" sign. After the war the voters stuck two fingers up to Mr Churchill – but didn't turn their hands around – when, in the 1945 election, they voted for a Labour government and a new Prime Minister.

What did Asquith say? If someone asks you a hard question like, "When are you going to make Bungee jumping compulsory for the Royal Family?" you can answer, "What did Asquith say?" Prime Minister Asquith always said, "Wait and see!" and this became such a favourite saying that when someone asked him a question everyone would chant the answer for him, "Wait and see!" But this is not a good answer to give if the question is, "Can you tell me the time, please?"

X The politician's favourite letter ... especially when you place it against his name on the voting paper. You can't put a tick or a circle on your ballot paper or write, "I want to vote for this politician because s/he's the best of this pathetic lot I've been given to choose from." It has to be a *cross* ... carried over from the days when most voters couldn't write their own names and signed everything with a cross.

Young fogey Teachers and parents are old fogeys – really boring people who never want to try any new ideas ... new ideas like having roast turkey on New Year's Day so the turkeys can have a happy Christmas. In the 1980s a new breed of politician were just as boring, but much younger. They became known as Young Fogeys and were usually Conservatives. Now there are Young Fogeys in every party.

Zeds (Also spelt Zzzzz.) This is what many politicians do in Parliament. Some sessions go on long into the night and some MPs simply drop off to sleep. If you are speaking at 2:00 am and you want people to notice you then it's an idea to scatter sharp tacks on those comfortable green leather benches. MPs have had a tax on people and a tax on houses and a tax on petrol. A tax on almost everything. You could be the first MP to have tacks on the seats in Parliament!

WHAT CHANCE HAVE YOU GOT?

Boring fact number 1:

There are 659 members of Parliament (529 from England, 40 from Wales, 72 from Scotland and 18 from Northern Ireland). What chance have you got of being one of them? Since there are 58 million people in Britain then your chances are 1 in 90,000. Of course, not *every* one of the 58 million wants to be in Parliament, so that increases your chances.

Boring fact number 2:

If you join one of the "Big Three" parties (Conservative, Labour or Liberal) then you can't just walk into a meeting and say, "I want to be your MP."

If you went to (say) the Conservative Party Office they would tell you, "There are another 600 to 800 people who *also* want to be a Conservative MP. Get in the queue!"

You would then have to trot off to your local Conservative Party Office and apply to be their MP.

If your local Conservative is pretty *sure* to be elected then it is known as a "safe" seat.[3] There are usually 250 to 350 people waiting for each nice "safe" Conservative seat. (Only the party pet politicians are going to be chosen for these.)

If there is likely to be a close contest then it is known as a "marginal" seat – and there are usually between 75 to 150 people waiting for the chance to fight that one. (Imagine the glory if you win!)

[3] A "seat" is a district. A Member of Parliament is supposed to look after everyone in his "seat". A "safe" seat is one where his party would have their MP elected even if a Barbary ape stood for election. Not to be confused with a stainless-steel toilet seat which is also a safe seat.

If your party has *no* chance of winning then it's a no-hope seat – but they don't call it that because they don't like to admit they have no hope. There are always 10 to 15 people waiting to be humiliated by losing this one. (But it's good practice to fight it so you'll know what you're doing when a "safe" seat comes along.)

But if you *really* want to increase your chances then aim to be the right sort of person...

Top tips 3 : How to succeed in getting into Parliament without really trying

Some people find it easier to get into Parliament than others. If you want the best chance of becoming your local Conservative MP then...

● Be male. Ever noticed there are equal numbers of women and men in Britain? Not in Parliament. Parliament is a big Boys' Club especially in the Conservative Party where only 13 of their MPs were women in 1997. If you want to join the Conservative "Boys' Club" it helps to be a feller.

POLLY'S THE NAME, MISTER POLLY.

● Be rich. Members of Parliament used to be rich enough to give up earning a living and enter Parliament instead. In the 19th century, members of Parliament were paid (very badly) so you could enter Parliament without starving. Now the large political parties (Labour, Liberal and Conservative) will help you fight an election. Joining the Conservatives will cost you £20 a year ... but if you want to slip them £100 or a few thousand they will be very grateful. They may even make you their MP!

- Be married. You will be judged by the company you keep and the family you come from. Having a partner who is a millionaire (like Margaret Thatcher's husband) does you no harm at all. A father who was a circus performer and a garden gnome-maker is not a great help − silly people tried to embarrass John Major by reminding him that's what his dad did. It's probably best to have no parents at all.

HOW EMBARRASSING, TO HAVE A PRIME MINISTER FOR A SON

- Be old. The average age of Conservative members is 62!
- Go to a public/independent school. Learn to talk posh, have plenty of posh friends in "high places". 78 of the Conservatives' 165 MPs in the 1997 election went to public/independent schools, (16 of those went to Eton).

There are many Members of Parliament who are *all* of these things. They represent voters many of whom are *none* of these things! This is, of course, very unfair. Potty, in fact.

Quick quote: "Leading the Conservative Party is like driving pigs to market." That was the view of Stanley Baldwin ... who led the Conservative Party! As Conservative MP Julian Critchley said in 1995, "The amazing thing about the Conservative Party is the amount we all hate each other."

If you went to the Labour Party, on the other hand, they are trying to make sure women have just as much chance to become MPs as men. In 1995 they even tried to force some places to choose a woman as their candidate but an industrial tribunal would not let them do that. So top tips to be selected as a Labour Candidate are...

- Be a woman. Labour had a plan to make half of their MPs women by around the year 2005. That's starting to look unlikely now, but at least 101 women were elected as Labour MPs in 1997.

- Come from a working class family. Only 13 of Labour's 418 MPs in 1997 went to public/independent schools ... and 47 were school teachers! (Why on earth give up a lovely job like that to be an MP?)

- If you cannot manage this then *invent* a working class background for yourself. Prime Minister Tony Blair was a lawyer, living in London and sending his kids to a posh grant maintained school. But his life history in the reference book *Who's Who* said his address, before becoming Prime Minister, was in Trimdon Station, a working-class pit village in Durham, and that he

was a member of Trimdon Village Working Men's Club. Tony Blair actually went to a public school and Oxford University. (Labour MP Tony Benn was born to the title Viscount Stansgate ... so he changed his name.)

- Be an "activist" – go around working for good causes ... "Child Poverty Action Group", "Campaign for Nuclear Disarmament" or even "The Badger Defence Union" (honest!). Maybe you could even invent your own "good cause" and be a megastar. Why not start the "Society for the Preservation of Hamsters in Hampstead" or "Action Against Footballers Spitting in Public".

- Be rich. But a Labour Party member doesn't splash money around like a Conservative. Use it to "buy" a few hundred party memberships and use those bought members to vote for you. This happened in Manchester Gorton in 1994. Unfortunately this is illegal and when someone tried it the plan didn't work. Some of the people who voted for the candidate did not exist! Others *had* existed but were disqualified from voting because they had been dead for a few years. (Remember: You cannot vote in a Parliamentary election if you are dead – this sensible rule stops candidates digging up graves and knocking on coffin lids to ask, "Are you going to vote for me?")

Quick quote: "Leading the Labour Party is like driving an old stage coach. If it's rattling along at a good speed, most of the passengers don't start quarrelling. As soon as it stops they start arguing about which way to go. The trick is to keep it going at great speed." (Harold Wilson ... leader of the Labour Party, of course.)

But don't worry if you don't fit into any of these categories. If you want to change things you have to give it a go...

WHAT'S THE BIG IDEA?

People become Members of Parliament for a few different reasons. They may be...

- Saints

  I WANT TO MAKE THE WORLD A BETTER PLACE TO LIVE IN.

- Power-mad

  I WANT TO RULE THE WORLD!

  VOTE FOR ME

- Greedy

  I WANT TO MAKE LOTS OF MONEY IN MY LIFE

  BECOMING AN MP IS JUST STEP ONE!

- Adventurous

  I'VE TRIED TIGER SHOOTING AND GAMBLING AT MONTE CARLO BUT THERE'S NO EXCITEMENT LIKE BEING IN THE HOUSE OF COMMONS.

(Lord Randolph Churchill MP.)

- Potty

  I WORK A 20 HOUR DAY AND SLEEP JUST FOUR HOURS.

  ZZZ

Which one are you?

Quick quote: "He knows nothing. He *thinks* he knows everything. He should be a politician." (Or a teacher?)
(Playwright and political thinker George Bernard Shaw.)

Of course, you may simply stand for Parliament because you have a "Great Idea" that you want people to share ... or something terrible is going on that you want to stop!

That's how Parliament started, really. A powerful Baron, called Simon de Montfort, had a "Great Idea". But be warned: it brought him a very messy death!

IT ALL STARTED WITH A GREEDY KING. YEAH, I KNOW ALL KINGS ARE GREEDY. WELL, THIS ONE WAS HENRY III OF ENGLAND. HEN USED TO BE A GOOD MATE — IN FACT I MARRIED HIS SISTER — BUT THEN HE STARTED WASTING HIS MONEY. WARS IN FRANCE, BUYING THE THRONE OF SICILY FOR ONE OF HIS SONS! WHERE WAS ALL THE MONEY COMING FROM? GUESS!

I WANT THE BARONS TO FORK OUT!

34

OF COURSE OLD HENRY BROKE HIS PROMISE, DIDN'T HE? SO WE WENT TO WAR WITH HIM. WE DID WELL AGAINST HIM TOO. WE WON THE BATTLE OF LEWES IN 1264 IF YOU LIKE BORING FACTS. I RAN THE COUNTRY AND SET UP THE FIRST PARLIAMENT.

CURSES, I'M A CAPTURED KING IN A COLD AND CREEPY CLINK

UNFORTUNATELY WE RECKONED WITHOUT HIS SON, YOUNG E.D. HE STUFFED US AT THE BATTLE OF EVESHAM, 4 AUGUST 1265.

OFF WITH DE MONTFORT'S HEAD!

AND HIS ARMS AND HIS LEGS!

THE KING AND THE BARONS MADE A LASTING DEAL. IT INCLUDED THE MONARCH CALLING PARLIAMENT TO HELP HIM RULE. EVERYONE CELEBRATED MY WONDERFUL INVENTION. EVERYONE EXCEPT ME THAT IS...

MY HEAD WAS SENT AS A GIFT TO THE WIFE OF MY ENEMY, ROGER MORTIMER

PRETTY DRASTIC HAIRCUT YOU HAVE THERE, SIMON! HEH HEH!

So, if you have a "Big Idea" in your head, be sure you have a head to keep it in.

MAD MANIFESTOS

If you *haven't* got an idea then borrow someone else's. Most Members of Parliament join one of the main parties – Conservative, Labour or Liberal. The parties tell their Members of Parliament what to think.

Party promises

- the Conservative Party – "You can only be sure with the Conservatives" (1997).
- the Labour Party – "New Labour because Britain deserves better" (1997).
- the Liberal Democrat Party – "Make the difference" (1997).

Voters watch their Party Political Broadcasts on television (if they can stay awake), listen to canvassers (if they don't slam the door on their foot), read the party adverts (if they can be bothered) and read the party manifestos (printed explanations of the policies the parties stand for).[4]

Voters should then be able to answer the following simple questions. You could try them out on your parents and teachers. They are always complaining that *you* don't listen ... just see how much *they've* listened to the adverts and broadcasts!

[4] You would think the parties would scatter their manifestos like confetti at a wedding. In fact it is difficult to get your hands on copies. Try your local library, try yellow pages, try your local council offices and find out just how difficult it is. You'd think the parties didn't *want* you to know what they stand for!

Who says that?

Either the Conservatives, the Labour Party or the Liberal Democrats said the following. Can you guess which party said what?

... improving education standards
... nursery education for everyone
... inspecting schools
... training teachers to be better
... better equipment for pupils to use
... more pay for teachers

Answer:
All the parties believe in all of these ideas! (Whether they will do them when they are in power is another matter.) There are some differences, of course. Labour makes the promise that "no child will have to use an outside lavatory". Thanks Labour, we appreciate that!

Potty political fact: How to get votes – literally!

To have a real chance of becoming an MP you have to join one of the main parties. But in June 1994 Richard Huggett came up with a brilliant new scheme that almost worked. (This is quite amazing since old Richard used to be a headteacher. Imagine that? A headteacher with a brilliant idea?)

The Devon election was between a Conservative and a Liberal Democrat. Old Richard called himself a "Literal Democrat".

Spot the difference? A lot of Devon voters didn't. 10,203 people voted for Richard Huggett ... more

than had ever voted for a one-man party before. The
Liberal Democrats lost by just 700 votes and were
furious. If they had got just 701 of the ex-
headteacher's votes they would have won!

They claimed the Devon voters had been confused
and voted for old Richard by mistake. The Liberal
Democrats failed to get the result changed.

Once you have an idea you must also be able to say
something about Education, Health, Defence and so
on. These ideas are written down in incredibly
boring booklets called *manifestos*. All the MPs in a
party are expected to stick to the manifesto. The
booklets also tell the *voters* what the party promises
to do if it gets into power.

This is a bit like your parents promising...

The cunning trick is to promise *anything*, get enough idiots to vote for you, get into power ... then *break* your promises! This happens at every election, whoever wins, and millions of voters fall for it every time! Potty!

Other election winners are just unlucky – like the 1939 Conservatives who promised peace but were forced to go to war. Governments can't tell what other countries are going to do.

You also need a good "slogan" – a few words that sum up your ideas in a catch phrase. Print them on strips of paper so people can stick them on to car bumpers or windows.

That has to be better than Chester Arthur, a US politician in the late 19th Century who promised...

40

Chester was President from 1881 till 1885. But when he used the *dinner pail* slogan, he lost!

Potty policies

You may have spotted the fact that Simon de Montfort did not belong to a political party. They came along 500 years later. He didn't have a written manifesto either. If he had it would have been...

Of course, if you do not like any of the big parties' "Big Ideas" then you will simply have to come up with an idea of your own and form your own party.

What would your manifesto be?

Of course you have to be prepared to defend your manifesto. Go to public meetings and answer any questions ...

Lousy laws

You may think that these are wild ideas. But politicians have passed some strange laws in the past. Pester your parents and show off your political power-brain. Ask them which of the following are potty but true and which are pottily false?

1. If workers have a meeting then it is against the law to talk about their wages. True/false?

2. A voter may break into a tax office if he has reason to believe that the office owes him money. True/false?

3. Every school must provide a hot meal for a pupil if he or she wants one. True/false?

4. An American can vote in a British election if s/he has lived in the country for more than 12 months. True/false?

5. Men who powder their wigs must pay extra tax on hair powder. True/false?

Answers:

1 True. A law passed at the beginning of the 19th century when the bosses were worried about their workers rioting and creating a revolution.

2 False. This idea WAS put forward by Conservative MP Nicholas Ridley but it never became law.

3 True. A law passed in 1906. Unfortunately the law forgot to say it had to be a tasty and well cooked meal. They let kids in for 90 years of lumpy mashed potato and bullet peas.

4 False. But a Briton living in America (or anywhere else in the world) can vote by post.

43

5 **True.** The law was introduced in 1795 by Prime Minister William Pitt because he needed money for the war against France. Four years later he invented the dreaded Income Tax which has been with us ever since.

Potty parties

Some parties don't have much of a manifesto. What they have instead is a *name*. Vote for that name and you know what you are getting. For example, in 1987 a candidate called W O Smedley created a party and stood for the "Common Market, 'No' – Hanging, 'Yes', Party" (and got 217 votes).

Pester your political pals with this question: How many of the following parties have actually stood for Parliament in the past 50 years?

Party	Year	True/false
1 Up The Creek Have A Party	1992	True/false
2 Blancmange Thrower	1987	True/false
3 Black Haired Medium Caucasian Male	1997	True/false
4 National Teenage Party	1963	True/false
5 Let's Have Another Party Party	1987	True/false

6 Mongolian Barbeque Great Place to Party	1997	True/false
7 Fancy Dress Party	1987	True/false
8 Elvisly Yours Elvis Presley Party	1984	True/false
9 Eurobean from the Planet Beanus	1994	True/false
10 Official Acne Party	1984	True/false

SORRY, I THOUGHT YOU SAID 'VENUS'.

EUROBEAN FROM THE PLANET BEANUS

Potty political answer

They are ALL names that people have given to their party ... and *you* thought Labour was a stupid name for a party!

Most of these candidates paid £500 for a bit of a laugh or to get publicity for their cause ... like the 1984 "No Increase In Dental Charges Party" or the

"Make Criminals Concerned About our Response To Hostility and Yobbishness (McCARTHY) Party".

But crazy as some of these people are, there are crazier people. There are people who actually *voted* for them.

The "Official Acne Party" candidate got only 15 votes in Chesterfield. (So the people of Chesterfield can walk the streets safely, knowing there are only 15 idiots in the area.) But the "Blancmange Thrower" got 328 votes in Windsor (where the blancmange eating Royal family have a palace). And the "Eurobean from the Planet Beanus Party" candidate got an amazing 1,106 votes in South Wales West Euro-Elections. If you ever go to South Wales watch out for Planet Beanus supporters. There are a lot of strange people around there ... at least 1,106! You have been warned!

Boring fact number 3
Once you have your manifesto you are ready to fight an election.

The big political parties spend at least £6 million pounds on an election campaign – sometimes as much as £20 million. This money helps to pay for things like Party Political Broadcasts on television, advertising, leaflets, balloons. Anything ... except bribing the voters; you are only permitted to bribe voters with your promises!

Potty political fact: More money than sense
Those rich Americans spend more on one candidate than the British do on a whole election. Michael Huffington spent his personal fortune of $25

million on his 1994 campaign to get into the Senate. He got 3,481,840 votes – that's over $7 for each vote – and he *lost* to an opponent who spent "only" $14 million.

Money comes from party funds – membership money, sponsors and special fund-raising events. Money-raising schemes are the best. If you want to raise a lot of money then why not hold a party at your local burger bar ... and charge everyone £10 a ticket to attend. (This is a bargain. Labour Party fund feasts cost £500 a ticket!)

The trouble with sponsors is that they expect something in return for their money. Labour MP Ann Clwyd was sponsored by The Transport and General Workers Union. The union members had one view on how the Labour Party should be run – Ann Clwyd had a *different* idea. She refused to support their ideas – *they* refused to give her any more money.

You also have to be very careful about accepting money from crooks. In the late 1980s the business-man Robert Maxwell gave the Labour Party money in the hope that they would win an election and do him a few favours when they got into power. When he died, and all his deals became public, the Labour Party felt they had to give the money back to the pensioners who lost their pensions because of him.

The Conservatives accepted almost £4 million from another fiddling fraudster called Asil Nadir. He was hoping that some of the crimes he was accused of would be overlooked – they weren't and he ran off home to Cyprus.

The best rule is: only accept money from honest people.

So, once you have your Big Idea and you have your manifesto, then you have to persuade people to vote for you!

SITTING AND STANDING

The country is divided into 659 areas and each area sends an MP to parliament. The areas are known as seats.

If you put yourself forward to be elected then you "stand" for Parliament.

Got it? Most people who have a seat *sit* on it. But an MP has to *stand* for a seat. Potty.

Of course, it would be very confusing if everybody decided to stand for a seat. So there is a law that is meant to put silly standers off. It is a law which says you must pay a "deposit" of £500. If five per cent of the voters in a seat (1,000 to 2,000 people) vote for you then you get your money back ... even if you lose the election. If *less* than five per cent vote for you then you lose your £500.

Even the big parties lose deposits ... in 1997 the Conservatives lost 8. They were lucky. The Referendum Party lost 505 (that's £252,500 if you don't have a calculator handy) and the Natural Law Party lost 196 deposits (£98,000).

So, the best way to get that £500 back is to make sure you win ... by fair means or foul.

WHERE DO I START?

I'm glad you asked me that. When an election is announced just go down to the local Town Hall and put your name down as the candidate for your party.

And pay the £500. Then you need to get the signatures of 10 voters to support you. That's to stop people wasting time by standing for election when they will get no votes at all!

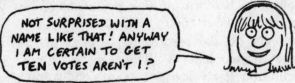

Not in Britain. But in the Bahamas in July 1977, Mr Wideon Pyfrom of the Free National Party got no votes at all.

Funny you should say that, but NO!

Potty political fact: Less than popular

Ten voters say they support you before you can stand for election. So it is difficult to get *less* than ten votes at the election. The following succeeded!

- 1997 Putney. D Vanbraam (Renaissance Democrat Party) – 7 votes.
- 1984 Chesterfield. J Connell (Peace Party) – 7 votes.

But the joint winners are:

- 1988 Kensington. Dr Kailish Trevadi (Independent Janata Party)

and ...

- 1982 Glasgow. Commander W Boaks (Public
  Safety Democratic Monarchist White Resident
  Party).[5]

  How many votes did these champion losers get? 6?
  5? 4? Or 3?

Answer:
5 votes ... so there is still a chance you can break
the British record!

[5]If you think his party has a funny name then what about The Christian
Socialist Opposing Secret Masonic Government Party?

CRAZY CANVASSING

When you set out to get voters to notice you then this is called "canvassing". Voters will not leave their cosy firesides, television soaps and fish suppers to come and listen to you.

You, the politician, must go to *them*. Walk the streets, knocking on doors...

Knocking on doors and persuading people to vote for you! Find out what their problems are and promise to solve them if they vote for you. Remember: you can always break your promise after you are elected.

Of course, you will not be welcome at every house. (Or *any* house, come to that!) Knocking on doors can even be dangerous at times. Remember: Rottweilers don't vote and they don't care which party you belong to. But they *do* believe in democracy and equality – so they bite *every* visitor *equally* hard.

Humans are just as dangerous. This is reflected in an old street song that kids used to sing…

VOTE, VOTE, VOTE FOR WINSTON CHURCHILL!
WHO'S THAT KNOCKING AT THE DOOR?
IF IT'S CHURCHILL LET HIM IN,
IF IT'S ATTLEE KICK HIS SHIN!
AND HE WON'T COME A-KNOCKING ANY MORE!

Naturally you swap the names around to suit the politician you support. A kick on the shin is one of the nicer welcomes you can expect in some areas!

One canvasser was attacked by a terrier. The owner of the house shouted, "Stop it, Jack!" to the terrier. Then the house owner spotted the canvasser was from a party he hated. "Get him, Jack!" he cried instead!

One candidate was a pop singer so he cruised the streets singing to the voters and playing his electric guitar. One group of people on a street corner signalled for him to shut up and pointed at a house. He sang even louder, and called, "Come on! Join in!" Then he saw the undertakers coming out of the house with a coffin. He had disturbed a funeral. (He was NOT elected!)

Nowadays many parties are playing safe and turning high-tech. They canvass voters by phone. Phones don't bite, kick or scratch.

Crazy candidates

What do you do if you are a voter and a candidate knocks on your door?

Slam the door in their face? No. They are used to that. There are *much* crueller ways to deal with unwanted canvassing candidates. So cruel that they may not call at your house for another 100 years (or until you are dead, whichever is the sooner).

Instead of shutting them out, invite them in! Then ask them questions ... and promise that you'll vote for them if they can prove that their political knowledge is so great they are worth your vote.

All they have to do is get 10 out of 10 in this **Potty Politicians Punishment Quiz.** (Or, if you're feeling really mean, you could make that 11 out of 10.)

1 Parliament used to be a group of men who came together to advise the monarch. They told him or her what people in their part of the country thought about things. But in Charles II's time Parliament began to split into "parties" for the first time. The King's supporters were called Tories by the opposition party, the Whigs. Conservatives today are still called "Tories" ... but what exactly does the word "Tory" mean?
a) It's short for "History" ... a "Tory" is a great believer in following the old ways from History
b) It is short for "*Story*-tellers" ... or liars. You can't call your enemy a liar in Parliament so you call him a story-teller, later shortened to story then to Tory
c) A Tory was an Irish cattle thief

2 The House of Commons has two tiers of benches facing each other. On the floor between the front benches there are two red lines. Speakers must never cross these lines. They are set a certain distance apart to stop trouble. What distance apart are they?

a) Two arms-lengths to prevent opponents punching one another

b) Two sword-lengths to prevent opponents fencing

c) The average spitting distance to prevent opponents spitting at one another (deliberately or accidentally when a speaker sprays his "s" sounds and says, "So sorry I soaked you, sir").

3 The chief ministers meet in a group called "The Cabinet". But how did this group get its name?

a) Charles II held meetings with his ministers in a small room called a "Cabinet"

b) The ordinary MPs used to drink ale, but the important ones met at a cabinet which held bottles of wine and brandy. To be invited to join the Cabinet group was an honour

c) Ordinary MPs walked to parliament. The important ones were driven in a carriage so they could talk privately. The carriage was a large cab, known in the 17th century as a Cabinet

4 Victoria's favourite Prime Minister, Benjamin Disraeli, once challenged a politician's son to a duel. When the young man refused Disraeli wrote him a letter and called him what insulting name?

a) A yahoo

b) A yob

c) A yak

5 In 1995 calves were being stuck in tiny crates and transported to Europe to be slaughtered. An MP wanted a new law to stop this – give the calves a comfortable trip ... then slaughter them. A Conservative MP, Peter Atkinson, wanted farmers who made money from selling calves to vote for him and so he didn't want a new law to go through. He kept talking all night till there was no time left for a vote. (This is called filibustering.) The new law was wrecked. But what did Peter Atkinson talk about?

a) He told the story of his life from the age of three

b) He read letters from all the farmers who supported him

c) He read all the names in a London phone book

6 Often everyone in Parliament wants to speak at once. The Speaker decides who can have a turn next. Sometimes you go a whole session and never get heard. But, if you want to raise a "Point of Order" (an objection about the way the debate is being run), you are *always* heard immediately. But how does the Speaker know you want to raise a Point of Order and not simply speak in the debate?

a) You raise two hands instead of one

b) You put a black top hat on your head and stand up

c) You shout out, "Point of Order! Point of Order!"

7 The Prime Minister lives at 10 Downing Street when he or she stays in London. The Prime Minister may ruthlessly sack ministers or plot wars against enemies from here. This sort of brutal politics is very well suited to the address. Why? What happened at 10 Downing Street before it became the home of Prime Ministers?

a) It was a site for Shakespeare's bloodthirsty plays

b) It was a site for public hangings

c) It was a site for cock fighting

8 Britain has had two Prime Ministers, father and son, called Pitt. (Imagine travelling abroad and saying, "Our leading politicians are the Pitts!") We have also been led by a Tory Wellington[6] – and the Labour Party used to be led by a Foot.[7] Our politicians have fairly ordinary names compared to a European country that was led by a man whose name meant "cabbage" in their language.

---

[6] The Duke of Wellington. Prime Minister in 1828–30 and 1834.
[7] Michael Foot became Labour Party leader in 1980 but only lasted till 1983 when Foot got the boot and never became Prime Minister.

Which country?
a) Germany – Chancellor Kohl
b) Russia – President Yeltsin
c) France – Jacques Chirac

9 Some politicians lead their party but never get to become Prime Minister. They lose an election and the party tries a new leader. The Labour Party has been led by 10 men who *never* became Prime Minister. The Conservative Party has been going a lot longer than Labour. How many Conservative Party leaders have never become Prime Minister?
a) Ten
b) Five
c) Two

10 How many MPs are chosen at each General Election?
a) 658 plus one Prime Minister who is not an MP
b) 659 in 1997
c) 659 in every election since 1832

1 c) The opposition members were called "Whigs" by the Tories. A Whig was a Scottish robber who usually murdered his victims.

2 b) This rule has been broken. Conservative Minister Michael Heseltine became so agitated that he not only crossed the line but grabbed the symbol of the Queen's power … the Royal Mace … and waved it threateningly at the Opposition.

3 a) The leader of the Cabinet was the Prime (or Chief) Minister. Given the number of boozy Prime Ministers who have held office perhaps answer "b" would be better … but it isn't!

4 a) A yahoo. This was a crude sort of person in the story *Gulliver's Travels*. Now you know!

5 c) Peter Atkinson was allowed to get away with this trick. Unfortunately, calves don't have the vote and can't vote him out of Parliament. If *you* became an MP you might like to change that! The record is Labour's John Golding who spoke for 11 and a quarter hours in 1983.

6 b) A top hat is always kept in the House of Commons for this purpose. But, in a 1990s debate there were several MPs all wanting to raise Points of Order. There were not enough hats to go around so MPs began making paper hats. They then had another debate to decide whether or not paper hats counted as Point of Order hats.

7 c) The back of the House was known as the Cockpit. The records of King James I show that there was a bill for "a new mat upon the Cockpit, being broken and torn with Cocks fighting there". If that's what they did to the mat, imagine what

more than at any other time – 707.
size and others have shrunk. In 1918 there were
through the years as some areas have grown in
There have been different numbers of MPs
10b) Not "**a**" because the Prime Minister is an MP.
more likely to be elected.
become a Conservative Party leader – you are
9 c) A tip for the top seems to be that you should
as a President.
though an African country had a Canaan Banana
... the only country in the world led by a vegetable
8 a) Kohl is German for "cabbage". Germany is
the cocks did to one another. Gruesome!

How did your candidate do?

Score 0–5 Stupid enough to be an MP.

Score 6–9 Too clever by half. Never vote for a person as clever as this.

Score 10 If your candidate gets 10 out of 10 and says, "Now you have to vote for me!" there is still a way out. Go back to question 10. "How many MPs are chosen at each General Election?" and if the candidate answers "659 in 1997" then say, "Name them!"

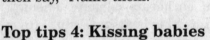

Top tips 4: Kissing babies

Politicians spend a lot of time kissing babies. This makes them look lovable. (The politicians, not the babies.) This is a disgusting and germ-spreading

60

activity. If you want to try it then sprinkle talcum powder and baby vomit on the back of your hand and practise kissing that. Always wear a surgical mask before trying it on real babies. A clothes peg on the nose is another excellent help in reducing the nauseating effect of nappy pong.

This may sound sick but, if you want to win, you will stop at *nothing*. Margaret Thatcher was photographed cuddling a calf ... and she got her picture in lots of papers and went on to win the election.

You have to do other things like visit hospitals ...

Visit old people's homes...

Potty political fact: A hair-raising experience

If you are a politician then don't lose your temper the way Conservative minister Leslie Hore-Belisha did in a Paris hotel in 1939.

In the middle of an argument a man grabbed Hore-Belisha's wig and flushed it down the nearest toilet. The wig was fished out of the hotel plumbing but Hore-Belisha refused to wear the soggy mat. (Wonder why?)

The minister left the hotel with a rug over his

head (saying he had a cold) and stayed out of sight
till the wig had been washed and curled and dried
again.

Top tips 5: Beat the system

You are only allowed to spend around £9,000 on your
campaign. Spend more and you will be disqualified.
So here's how to cheat:

VILE VOTERS

Everyone over the age of 18 has a vote. (Everyone except members of the House of Lords, criminals and lunatics, that is. This is a little odd, considering some of the crooks and lunatics who have become MPs!)

Potty political fact:

When voters come to put their cross on the voting sheet the names of the candidates are listed in alphabetical order. If you want to get to the top of the list then change your name to Aaron ... or Aardvark! Voters who can't make their minds up will give you their vote! Thousands of them!

The fact is there were 21 MPs elected in 1997 whose name began with "A". There were only two whose names began with "Y".

And voters may vote with an "X" ... but they never vote *for* an "X". There are *no* MPs with a name beginning with "X".

All your over-18 friends can vote for you. Of course, all your over-18 *enemies* can vote for the opposition. Your enemies might be pretty vile, in fact, but if you want to be an MP you have to suffer them ... and keep smiling.

It hasn't always been this way, of course. In the beginning *no one* had a vote. Just the monarch. The king or queen could say, "Tax this – tax that – spend the money on this – give my friends that. Kill him – let her go. Make war on them ... then go out and die for your country."

In time people got a bit fed up with miserable monarchs bossing them about. They wanted a *vote*. If they were rich enough and powerful enough then they could force the king to give them a say. Of course the only people with that sort of power were the barons. That's how it all started.

Boring fact number 4: Voters' time line

1213 King John invites four knights from each county to come and meet him for a chat about how to run the country. This was a BIG mistake. The knights get to like this taste of power.

1215 Grumpy John is forced to agree to the Magna Carta giving power to his lords.

1265 Henry III goes back on the promises made in Magna Carta and his barons capture him. Boss Baron Simon de Montfort not only invites knights to his new "Parliament" – he invites four ordinary people from each county too. Ordinary, but rich, of course.

1293 First mention of a Scottish Parliament. It's really a sort of court for the king and his council to sit in judgement.

13th century Edward I calls 50 Parliaments in his 35-year reign. But only 12 have commoners in them. Even then the commoners weren't too keen to attend. They knew they were only going so the king could demand money from them!

14th century The commoners become more powerful. If the king wants their taxes then they want something from the king in return – power.

15th century Every man with property worth 40 shillings can vote for his county commoner to go to Parliament. Trouble is there aren't many Parliaments to go to. Scotland has regular elections but just a few members run the whole show while the rest go home!

16th century Henry VIII likes the Commoners' Parliament. He can boast that they support his dreadful deeds – killing queens and robbing monasteries. More towns send commoners to Parliament to join the county men. Henry sells them the monastery

lands – in return they make Henry head of the church (instead of the Pope).

17th century Charles I tries to snatch back power from Parliament. He doesn't call Parliament for years. When he needs money he calls them. They refuse to give it to him unless they can meet regularly. Seems fair but Charlie disagrees. They make war on him and win. Charles gets the chop.

1707 The Treaty of Union joins Scotland to England. Scotland can now send members to a united Parliament. It's along a muddy road for Scottish members to get there ... but that Parliament is in London, not Edinburgh (which seems a bit unfair on Scots).

1832 The Great Reform Act lets more people vote, but they can't vote in secret and they can't vote on paper. They tell a voting official who they want to vote for and he marks it down. Everyone knows who they were voting for.

1842 A group called the Chartists have demonstrations (well, *riots* sometimes) to get votes for every man. They have a huge petition – unfortunately signed by jokers with names like Queen Victoria!

1858 Votes for men over 21 *if* they own some property – tramps get no vote. That's still just a quarter of all men. A few women are bothered by this, but not enough to make a big fuss ... yet.

1872 Secret voting at last. Now ballot-box bullies can't beat you up if you don't vote their way.

1881 Votes for women ... but only those in the Isle of Man.

1917 Women have been helping to win World War I. Their reward is to get the vote ... but only if they are over 30. All men over 21 get the vote – even if they have no property. Tramps celebrate!

1969 Kids of 18 years can vote now. Where will it all end? Votes for school pupils? Why not? They can't do much worse than the grown-ups!

Potty political fact: Crossed out crossers

Now nearly everyone has the vote. But the following people *cannot* become an MP:

- Aliens ... no this does not mean Martians or Extra-terrestrials. "Aliens" here means people who are not *British*.

- A traitor or someone in prison for more than a year. But you can keep your seat if you are sent to prison *after* you are elected.
- Certain persons suffering from mental illness. Some of our monarchs (certainly Henry VI and George III) were mentally ill. This didn't stop them from becoming king.
- Lords and Ladies. They have to give up their lordliness (or ladiness) and become a "commoner".
- Bankrupts. If you're broke you can't stand for Parliament. But, if you're broke, you probably can't afford to stand anyway.
- Judges, police officers and members of the armed forces. So one MP can *make* the laws then enforce them. No MP can vote to start a war then fight in it!

SUFFERING SUFFRAGETTES

One group of people who did not have the vote for hundreds of years was women.

In the 19th century they decided it was about time they had a say in making the laws that they had to live with. But it took a lot of arguing, fighting, suffering and even dying to get votes for women.

A National Union of Women Suffrage Societies was formed in 1897 ... but they were too polite and men were able to ignore them! Soon a group decided to use more extreme methods to get their views noticed.

Some of their actions were against the law and the women found they were arguing with the police as much as with the government. Suffrage means the right to vote – suffering may have been a better word for what these heroines went through.

Did you know...?

1 One of the early leaders was Christabel Pankhurst. Christabel was a polite woman who wanted to go to prison to draw attention to the Suffragette cause. She tried to punch a policeman but he grabbed her hands and she was not strong enough to free herself. She then decided to spit in his face ... but polite ladies do *not* spit, so Christabel had never learned how to do it. She failed in her attempt to spit! The police arrested her anyway and she went to prison when she refused to pay a fine.

2 A battle-cry of the Suffragettes was "Parliament or prison" ... and for many it was prison. When they got there they had all their clothes taken away and were dressed in prison uniform: patched and

stained underwear, rough wool stockings which kept falling down, and an uncomfortable dress stamped all over with broad arrows to show the world they were prisoners. At night they had to sleep on a bed that was nothing more than a plank.

3 Suffragette prisoners often refused to eat. These "hunger strikes" were aimed at forcing the government to change the law or watch the women die. The government ordered that the women be force-fed. The prisoner was strapped to a bed, a wood or metal "gag" was placed in the mouth to stop her closing it, a tube was pushed down the throat and into the stomach. Then a thin porridge was poured down the tube till the stomach was full. This painful process often seriously injured the prisoner.

4 Some women resisted the force-feeding. Emmeline Pankhurst, Christabel's mother, threatened warders with the only weapon she had in her cell ... a toilet pot! Emily Wilding-Davison barricaded herself into her cell so the warders could not get to her and force-feed her. Instead they pushed a hose pipe in the window of the door and flooded the cell with icy water till she was forced to give in. Then Emily threw herself under the hooves of the king's race-horse as it ran in the 1913 Derby. She was taken to the local hospital where police were called in to protect her from a mob that wanted to hang her. They could have saved themselves the trouble. She died from her injuries a few days later.

5 It wasn't only convicted prisoners who were roughly treated. On 18 November 1910 a group of 450 women marched to Parliament to meet the Prime Minister. He refused to see them and as they tried to march onward the police started using new and vicious tactics. They were determined to hurt the women as much as possible before arresting them. They were knocked to the ground or tripped. The police did very little to stop trouble-makers in the crowd rushing in to punch or kick those on the ground. The day became known as "Black Friday".

6 Other Suffragette meetings were also wrecked by men. They threw tomatoes, flour and *mice* ... alive and dead! Others hurled a disgusting collection of fish-heads soaked in pee. At London's Albert Hall a woman was beaten with a horse whip and had a lighted cigar pushed on to her wrist as she tried to attend a meeting.

7 In 1907 women were chaining themselves to the railings outside government offices. In 1909, ten of them climbed on to the roof of a hall where the Prime Minister was trying to make a speech – they used axes to hack off slates and throw them down into the hall. By 1912 the Suffragettes had discovered a new way of breaking the law. They began

HOW'S THAT FOR A HOLE IN ONE ?

pushing burning rags into pillar boxes to destroy the post. This then grew into setting fire to government offices and even a castle. Key-holes were stuffed up with lead pellets, railway carriage seats slashed and men's most sacred places wrecked when golf courses were dug up!

8 Some Suffragettes tried incredibly clever ideas to get to the Prime Minister to argue their case. Two women wrapped themselves in brown paper, had themselves weighed and stamped at the post office and waited to be collected as parcels. They were addressed to the Prime Minister's home, 10 Downing Street. The post office, sadly, refused to deliver them. Another used a cunning weapon to try to burn down the Dublin Theatre Royal ... a handbag filled with gunpowder. This Guy Fawkes in a skirt did a little damage ... which is still more than Guy himself managed.

9 Suffragettes even died for the right to vote. Two died from injuries received on Black Friday as well as Emily Wilding-Davison's death at the Derby.

10 Women did such a valuable job in helping Britain win the 1914–18 war that men felt they had at last deserved the vote. In 1918 married women over 30 were allowed to vote and the first women stood for Parliament. Christabel Pankhurst lost in her attempt to become an MP. The first woman MP was Lady Astor who, strangely, was *not* a Suffragette. In June 1928 women over 21 were given the vote, making them equal at last to men. And as that law was passed in Parliament, the great Suffragette leader Emmeline Pankhurst was being buried.

TAKING YOUR SEAT

Congratulations! You have been elected as a Member of Parliament.

What do you do next? You go to the Houses of Parliament. But be careful! Make sure you go in the right door!

Westminster has over 100 rooms, 100 staircases and over three kilometres of corridors!

I'M LOST! CAN YOU DIRECT ME TO DISRAELI'S OFFICE?

Potty political fact:
Westminster was a royal palace that the monarchy allowed Parliament to meet in. In the end Parliament took it over. The politicians used to vote with sticks. In 1854 a pile of old sticks caught alight and set fire to Westminster Palace. They succeeded where Guy Fawkes had failed! The present Houses of Parliament were built in its place.

Did you notice that it is called *Houses* not *House*? There are *two* of them.

The Lords meet in the *House of Lords*. Members of Parliament meet in the *House of Commons*.

Common. That's you. (Unless you are a lord or a lady reading this in which case I offer you my humble and grovelling apology your high and mighty worshipfulness!)

You may be common, but as an MP you can do something the Queen can't do. What is it?

75

Charles I once marched through that door and tried to arrest some troublesome MPs. (They knew he was coming so they ran away!)

Ever since then the monarch has been banned. When the Queen opens Parliament every year she sends a messenger called Black Rod to knock on the door. He is dressed in quaint old clothes and guess what he carries in his hand? Yes! Award yourself a coconut if you said "a black rod". (How did you guess?)

Black Rod knocks on the door to the Commons (with his Black Rod, naturally) and invites the Commons up to the House of Lords where they all squeeze in.

As a new MP do not show yourself up at the opening by asking,

WHICH ONE'S THE QUEEN THEN?

When she opens Parliament she is wearing her best crown and sitting on the throne at the end of the hall. A blind-folded man on a flying horse couldn't miss her.

The Lord Chancellor sits on something called The Woolsack. This is a sign of wealth (from the days when Britain made its money from the wool trade) – it is not a sign that he can't afford a decent chair. Otherwise the House of Lords looks like the House of Commons but with red leather on the benches where the Commons have green.

76

And so the Queen makes a speech – a bit like launching a ship really – except they aren't her words. She is just reading out what the government of the time want her to say. When she finishes you trot back to the Commons and start your business.

Potty political fact:
In 1900 there was a general election. In 243 of the 670 seats there was no choice – only one candidate stood for election. That means only one-third of the men (and none of the women) had any chance to use their vote!

Terrible timetable
In school everyone has a timetable so they know who is where, when. MPs have a timetable but it has one important difference. You HAVE to go to school. You DON'T have to go to the House of Commons every day.

Of course the House is open for business most days. You can wander in and out of the debates whenever you like but this is the usual timetable.

1 Morning: Go to your office, answer letters and phone calls.

2 2:25 pm: A policeman cries out … "Speeeeeee-aker!" … then the door keeper enters dressed in smart silk stockings and white gloves…

He is followed by the Serjeant-at-Arms carrying the great Royal mace, an ornamental club…

Behind them walks the boss of the Commons, the Speaker.[8]

Then come the Chaplain and the Secretary followed by the MPs.

3 2:30 pm: The Chaplain says prayers.

For the next hour the MPs talk about the laws they plan to pass. These are written down and called "Bills".

---

[8]The Prime Minister may be in charge of the Government like the manager of a football team. But here, on the field of play, the Speaker is the referee. S/he's in charge, sorts out squabbles and keeps the boisterous "players" in order. In 1995 Betty Boothroyd became the first woman Speaker.

78

NOT TO BE CONFUSED WITH A RESTAURANT BILL OR A BLACKBIRD'S BILL.

A Bill has three "Readings" in Parliament. First it's just read out. After the second reading it's talked about, argued about and sent to small committees of MPs to change. After the third reading it goes to the House of Lords[9]. The Queen then says "OK" and it's law. These three readings can take a year or so.

4 3:00 pm: For half an hour (Wednesdays only) everything stops. It's Prime Minister's question time. Main questions are sent to the Prime Minister two weeks in advance. Some of these are soft questions which just allow him to waffle.

CAN YOU LIST YOUR APPOINTMENTS FOR TODAY, SIR, MY DEAR PRIME MINISTER?

CREEP!

But "supplementary" questions can be asked and they can be really nasty ...

IS IT TRUE THAT YOUR GOVERNMENT PLANS TO PUT A TAX ON BREATHING?

CURSES! SHE'S GUESSED THE TRUTH!

5 3:30 pm: Back to the debates. But the best television shots of the day have been taken. No one will notice if you disappear unless ...

IT'S A **THREE LINE WHIP!**

---

[9]They may be a bit awkward and ask for changes, in which case it may go backwards and forwards between the Houses like a yo-yo.

Glad you mentioned that. MPs are told which debates to attend by their Party "Whips". These are bully boys who make sure you do what your *Party* wants and don't go voting for the things that *you* like! The lists of debates have lines drawn underneath them...

WE WOULD BE JOLLY PLEASED IF YOU COULD ATTEND THIS DEBATE, OLD CHAP, IF IT'S NOT TOO MUCH TROUBLE.

THIS IS ACTUALLY QUITE IMPORTANT AND WE'D LIKE TO SEE YOU THERE.

DRAMATIC MUSIC AND ROLL OF DRUMS...

BE THERE **OR ELSE**. NOTHING SHORT OF DEATH IS ACCEPTED AS AN EXCUSE. LET US DOWN AND YOU ARE OUT OF THE PARTY, MUSH!

6 10:00 pm[10]: End of the day ...

UNLESS IT'S AN IMPORTANT DEBATE THAT HASN'T BEEN FINISHED. THEN IT CAN GO ON ALL NIGHT!

Potty political fact:

Parliament only meets on about 170 days every year! The rest of the time it's on holiday.

Schools meet on about 200 days a year. Which would you rather do?

MPs complain that they have all-night sessions but they are quite rare now. The longest ever ran from 4 pm on 31 January 1881 and didn't finish till 9:30 am on 2 February!

[10]Except on a Friday when Parliament sits from 9:30 am till 2:30 pm then everyone knocks off early and goes home for the weekend.

PARLIAMENTARY POLITENESS

In school you are supposed to call a teacher, Mr Smith, Miss Smith, Mrs Smith, Sir or Miss. You should NOT say, "Hoy, you with the ginger hair!" or "Albert, me old mate," or "Four-eyes" ... no matter *what* you call them behind their backs!

Parliament is just the same. You have to use the right words when speaking to people in a debate. Here are the important ones:

Who they are:	What you call them:
An enemy MP	The Honourable Member for X
An MP on your own side	My Honourable Friend, the Member for X
A Privy Councillor[11]	My Right Honourable Friend
A former soldier	The Honourable and Gallant Member
A Queen's Counsel[12]	The Honourable and Learned Member
A "Sir"	The Honourable and Noble Member

Practise on your school friends. "I say, may I borrow your ruler, My Honourable Friend the

[11] A Privy Councillor – a very high-up MP
[12] A Queen's Counsel – a very high-up lawyer as well as an MP

Member for Pottery Row?"

This is easier than being in Parliament and talking to a soldier who became a lawyer then an MP promoted to Privy Councillor. You will have to say to him:

MAY I ASK MY RIGHT HONOURABLE, LEARNED AND GALLANT FRIEND THE MEMBER FOR PUDDINGMINSTER ... ER, I FORGOT THE QUESTION!

The good news is you can call him "Fred" when you meet him in the pub!

Potty political fact: Naughty names 2

The Right Honourables have their titles, they have their proper names ... and some of them have nicknames.

A Conservative minister in the 1990s was Michael Heseltine. He earned the nickname "Tarzan" because of his flowing blond hair. He then tried to live up to his name by going ape in the House of Commons! In a fierce debate in 1975 he leapt from his seat, grabbed the Royal mace from the table between the benches and waved it at the enemy. His friends thought this was great and cheered like football hooligans!

AS LONG AS NO-ONE NICKNAMES ME 'HESELTINE'.

In 1988 MP Ron Brown tried the same thing but dropped it on the floor. He got jeers instead of cheers. He also got a repair bill for £1,000. Mr Brown's nickname is not recorded.

PERHAPS IT SHOULD BE 'PLONKER'?

Test your teacher

Teachers are usually older than pupils so they should know more about politics. Find the nearest teacher (or some other wrinklie) and ask them to match the nicknames to the real names of the following politicians. Only give them a clue if they ask for it ...

Nickname	Clue	Real name
1 Beast of Bolsover	Skins MPs alive?	a Edward Heath
2 Gorgeous	Gee-Gee perhaps?	b Michael Allison
3 The Grocer	Also a sailor!	c Margaret Thatcher
4 Jolly Jack	Until he got caught?	d David Lightbrown
5 The Iron Lady	And she was proud of it	e David Maxwell Fyffe
6 The Saint	St of Marks & Spencer	f Dennis Skinner
7 Dai Bananas	Not from Fife	g George Thomas

8 Mam's Boy	Wet Welshman	**h** Virginia Bottomley
9 The Terminator	A Whip who "tans" MPs?	**i** George Galloway
10 Elegant	Top-ly as well	**j** John Profumo

Answer:
1 – f)   2 – i)   3 – a)   4 – j)   5 – c)
6 – b)   7 – e)   8 – g)   9 – d)   10 – h)

Potty political fact: Definitely yes *and* no

When a debate is finished the MPs all go into one of two rooms to vote – "Aye" or "Nay" – Yes or No.

But if an MP is too tired or too stupid to go into the right one first time he can be dragged out by the Whips to vote on the other side. In fact one politician can vote "Yes" and "No" on the same question. Potty!

This would be a very handy thing to do in school…

Parliamentary impoliteness

Not every politician can *stay* polite. Some have come up with some pretty nasty remarks about Honourable Members … and even about Honourable Friends.

Note: Winston Churchill talking about Clement Attlee ... who beat him in the 1945 General Election! Baa!

Note: Winston Churchill's remark to Labour MP Bessie Braddock ... but maybe he didn't say it!

Note: Winston Churchill to Lady Astor ... but maybe he didn't say that either!

4 When you are in Parliament you are not allowed

to call another MP "drunk". In 1974 James Wellbeloved got around this problem ...

5 Denis Healey was the Labour Chancellor looking after Britain's economy between 1974 and 1979. Conservative Geoffrey Howe attacked Denis Healey's speech in the Commons and Healey rose with a smile on his face.

Denis Healey also referred to Mrs Thatcher as "Winston Churchill in a dress". But it was "Dead Sheep" Howe who made such a vicious speech against his leader, Mrs Thatcher, that the Conservatives sacked her as Prime Minister soon afterwards. Some sheep!

6 Modern politicians are a bit tame compared to the Victorians. Benjamin Disraeli did not just insult his enemies' ideas – he was very personal too.

LORD PALMERSTON IS AN OLD AND PAINTED PANTALOON, VERY DEAF, VERY BLIND. HIS FALSE TEETH WOULD FALL OUT OF HIS MOUTH WHEN HE SPEAKS, EXCEPT HE HESITATES SO MUCH WHEN HE TALKS.

7 People from the House of Lords are not above insults either. A trouble-maker was arguing with Lord Soper in a public meeting about Soper's religion:

CHRISTIANITY HAS BEEN ON THE EARTH 2000 YEARS AND LOOK AT THE STATE OF THE WORLD TODAY!

WATER HAS BEEN ON THE EARTH EVEN LONGER THAN THAT – AND LOOK AT THE COLOUR OF YOUR NECK!

8 The 1980s Labour Leader Neil Kinnock could be especially spiteful about his Conservative enemies. He said of Conservative minister Norman Tebbitt...

"He is like a boil on a verruca" ... while Education Minister Mark Carlisle was ...

A MOUSE LEARNING TO BECOME A RAT.

9 And talking of rats, they are the animals that are supposed to desert a sinking ship. And when John Major's Conservative Government looked like sinking at the end of 1995, one of his MPs, Alan Howarth, deserted to the Labour Party and another, Emma Nicholson, to the Liberal Democrats. Emma Nicholson held a seat in the west of England, so naturally one of her old MP "friends" labelled her ...

10 The art of potty political insults is as strong as ever. Here are some of the best from Tony Banks, Labour MP in the 1990s:

"She is a half-mad old bag lady." (Margaret Thatcher.)

"She is about as environmentally friendly as the bubonic plague." (Margaret Thatcher)

"I would be happy to see her stuffed, mounted, put in a glass case and left in a museum." (Margaret Thatcher.)

"The news that he had resigned worried me. If he jumped from Number 11 Downing Street there would now be a very large hole in the road." (Tubby Chancellor of the Exchequer Nigel Lawson.)

"Almost a complete waste of space." (Environment Secretary, Nicholas Ridley.)

These are the sort of witty words you need to learn if you are going to become an MP. The speakers probably practised them at their schools when they were in the playground. Unfortunately, they never grew up.

Of course these are only *words*. Blows are much more painful. During the 1960s the young Northern Ireland MP Bernadette Devlin crossed the floor of the House of Commons and smacked Conservative Reginald Maudling several times on the head. Another MP commented she was, "Like the 1849 Potato Famine – one of Ireland's natural disasters!"

POTTY POLITICAL SPEAKING

When you speak in Parliament you cannot make the mistake of saying what you mean. Politicians NEVER say what they mean.

Can you match the following words with their hidden meaning:

This...	really means...
1 You are imaginative	a You are a right clever clogs
2 That is a novel idea	b We had a terrible row
3 You have formidable talent	c I'll tell you a pack of lies
4 In all honesty	d You are potty
5 We had a frank and full discussion	e That's a load of rubbish

FRANKLY, WITH RESPECT, I THINK YOU'RE FORMIDABLY IMAGINATIVE

HOW DARE YOU?!!

Answer:
1d) 2e) 3a) 4c) 5b)

And if you really dislike an idea, you have *no* respect for the idea or the speaker then, of course, you say, *"With* respect…"

WITH RESPECT, MOTHER, CLEANING MY BEDROOM IS A NOVEL IDEA BUT YOU ARE CLEARLY IMAGINATIVE IF YOU THINK I'M GOING TO AGREE WITHOUT A FULL AND FRANK DISCUSSION.

Potty political fact: I spy, spies!

A new custom grew in the early 1940s when MPs were worried that German spies might be watching and listening from the public seats in the House of Commons. An MP could stand up and cry, "I spy strangers!" At that cry the House of Commons would be cleared for about 20 minutes and a break taken while the public were sent out.

There are not a lot of German spies around these days but an MP can still shout, "I spy strangers" and get the place cleared. In fact they only do this now to try and waste time or spoil a debate. No one has thought of putting a stop to this silly game. Potty!

Top tips 6: Parliamentary prattle

People go into Parliament to talk. They do *not* go there to listen to *you* talk. When you make a speech they will probably nod off to sleep, make paper darts with their order papers or chat to the MP next to them. This is very much the sort of behaviour you would expect from bored kids in a classroom with a terrible teacher.

But this is a great advantage to you in Parliament! Just like Mr Terrible Teacher you can talk the most senseless drivel ... and the chances are *no one will even notice!*

But just in case you *do* want people to listen to you then take a tip from the first Labour MP, Keir Hardie. When he arrived to take his seat in Parliament he was wearing a sweat-stained work suit (so they could smell him coming) ... and he was accompanied by a noisy brass band! For some reason they were playing the French National Anthem.

Silly speeches

Now that you have learned the important words and phrases of potty political speaking you are ready to make your first speech in Parliament.

The bad news is that it is against the rules to *read* your speech. You have to either learn it from memory or make it up as you go along. Other rules say:

MPs must stand up to speak.[13]

---

[13]Note that ministers often cheat and read statements prepared by their secretaries!

They must be bare-headed unless they are a woman. A woman MP can wear a hat.

> **Quick quote:** "There are three golden rules for Parliamentary speakers: Stand up. Speak up. Shut up." (J W Lowther, Speaker of the House of Commons 1917.)

Look at some of these examples of politicians' prattle from Britain and America. Real live politicians got away with this ... so why shouldn't you?

1 "London beat the racists in Tower Hamlets and the rest of the party proud of you doing it were and we much talk about outside the rest of London." John Prescott (then Deputy Leader of the Labour Party) said these words in 1995 and was cheered. When you see them written down you realize they are in fact nonsense.

2 And, if you didn't understand that, John Prescott went on to explain, "Let us say something to the unemployed, yes you are after full employment years and we can go back forward now back to full employment." (It might be a good idea to go back forward now back to the next example.)

3 President George Bush and his Vice-President,

Dan Quayle, were probably the Laurel and Hardy of silly speeches. Can you make sense of George Bush's remark: "You're burning up time. The meter is running through the sand on you." Or his, "Please don't look part of the glass, the part that is only less than half full." Vice-president Quayle said that someone leaving the White House staff, "isn't a man leaving with his head between his legs." Got that? As Dan Quayle himself said, "What a waste it is to lose one's mind … or not to have a mind is very wasteful." Quite right, Dan. Can you imagine a conversation between Dan Quayle and John Prescott?

HI, I'M DAN QUAYLE!

YES, WE MUCH TALK ABOUT YOU OUTSIDE LONDON BACK FORWARD NOW BACK...

4 Even when some British politicians make sense it is nonsense: "Motorway Intersection Six is still being planned. We aren't quite sure where but I imagine it would be between Intersection Five and Intersection Seven". Spokesman for the Department of Transport.
5 Really clever politicians can use words like knives to insult someone. Would you like to call someone, "A big mouth with a big head"? Victorian Prime Minister Disraeli insulted his enemy

Gladstone with an insult that means just that: "He is a sophisticated rhetorician, inebriated with the exuberance of his own verbosity and gifted with an egotistical imagination!" (Never mind what it means – just *learn* it!)

6 Of course, there are more ways than one of making a silly speech. Sometimes you can get away with saying something quite stupid. In 1932 the Conservative Prime Minister Stanley Baldwin said, "There is no power on earth that can protect you from being bombed. The bomber will always get through. The only defence is offence, which means you have to kill more women and children more quickly than the enemy if you want to save yourselves." Unfortunately, most British people believed him and in the Second World War seven years later they tried out this idea. Potty.

7 Sometimes politicians say something so clever it is silly ... and so silly it is clever. A US politician called Haldeman said, "Once the toothpaste is out of the tube it is awfully hard to get it back in." Try saying that to your friends. They will either a) agree, b) disagree or c) phone for men in white coats to wrap you up in a cosy little strait-jacket.

8 British politicians can say things equally weird. James Maxton had the brilliant idea of being in *two* parties at the same time in 1934. Not many politicians have thought of that one! When he was told he couldn't be in two at once he replied with the brain-numbing statement: "All I say is, if you can't ride two horses you have no right to be in the circus." A great writer like William Shakespeare couldn't have put it better.

9 Even the cleverest politicians can get *too* clever though. US President John Kennedy went to Berlin in 1963. He wanted to show off and speak German so he declared, "Ich bin ein Berliner." He *meant* "I am a Berliner!" ... but he got it wrong. In German his words actually mean, "I am a piece of sweet, sticky cake!"

10 Another unfortunate US President was Abraham Lincoln. He too opened his mouth and put his foot in it when he thought he was saying something very wise. Lincoln said, "The ballot is stronger than the bullet." Unfortunately there wasn't a *ballot* in sight when an assassin's *bullet* hit him behind the ear.

Potty political fact: No questions asked
Politicians can be incredibly lazy and yet stay in Parliament, election after election. Captain Henry Kerby was said to have asked only three questions in his time as an MP. Two were written questions and the third was, "Could somebody please open a window?" He was Arundel and Shoreham MP from 1954 and survived 17 years. Even after 17 years he wasn't voted out ... he died. (Death has only one vote ... but it usually counts more than a 20,000 majority.)

SHOCKING SCANDALS

When you are an MP then the public is watching you very closely to see that you behave yourself. A bit like walking round school with a sign saying: "Watch this pupil!"

Many of those people are jealous and can't wait for you to do something naughty so they can pretend to be shocked and write to the newspapers and demand that you resign.

Politicians never learn! They still do silly things and still get into trouble. Here are a few of the pottiest...

1 John Wilkes, MP 1757–1764. Wilkes was a newspaper owner who wrote such nasty things about King George III and Prime Minister Bute that he was thrown into jail. Wilkes became an MP and was thrown out of Parliament after being found guilty of fighting a duel. His opponent took his place even though Wilkes got more votes! Wilkes was also said to have joined the Hellfire Club where members held wild devil-worshipping parties. When he calmed down a bit he became respectable and Lord Mayor of London. John Wilkes survived the scandal – the Hellfire Club didn't!

2 Lloyd George. He was Chancellor of the Exchequer in the Liberal government in 1909. Then *The People* newspaper wrote a shocking story about Lloyd George having a girlfriend as well as a wife. Even worse, the girlfriend was married too! In 1909 this was a disgrace. Lloyd George took *The People* newspaper to court and sued them for telling such a damaging story about him. Lloyd George's wife backed him up and the crafty politician won ... even though the story about the girlfriend was true. Lloyd George took the usual oath in court; he swore on *The Bible*, "I promise to tell the truth, the whole truth and nothing but the truth," ... then he told a pack of lies. He went on to become Prime Minister. If liars can become politicians then great liars can become Prime Ministers.

3 Lloyd George (again!). When Lloyd George became Prime Minister he thought up a jolly good scheme to raise money. He would offer a rich person a title ... and the rich person would pay Lloyd George – £10,000 for becoming "Sir Something" and up to £50,000 for a really top title. He gave out 274 titles in just 18 months (that's one title every couple

of days); he created the Order of the British Empire (OBE) and gave out 25,000 in four years (nearly 20 a day!) and some said he made a million pounds for himself. A committee was then set up to make sure that people get honours because they are "fit and proper persons" and not because they are rich.[14]

4 John Profumo. Before you get the idea you can get away with everything the way Lloyd George did, take a look at what happened to Conservative John Profumo. He was the Minister for War and he had a girlfriend called Christine Keeler. But Christine had another boyfriend ... a Russian spy! Britain's war secrets could be passed to the Russians because of John Profumo's carelessness. When he was found out he lied to Parliament and was proved to be a liar. He had to resign. John Profumo did *not* survive – and neither did the Ministry of War. It became the Ministry of Defence. (Same thing, different name. Potty.)

5 Fergus Montgomery. Fergus was feeling a bit tense. He was suffering from "stress" – lots of MPs say this. (It makes you wonder why they don't give it all up and have an easier life – lion tamer, stunt man, bomb-disposal expert or teacher.) Anyway, Fergus took a calming tablet called a mogadon (and washed it down with a few glasses of whisky). In a happy state he then went out, picked up a couple of books from a bookshop and walked out ... without paying! He was charged with shop-lifting but

[14]But in 1992 seven out of 12 knighthoods to industry chiefs went to men whose company had given over £50,000 to the Conservative Party. In the 1996 New Year Honours a knighthood went to a man who just happened to have "loaned" the Conservative Party £4,000,000!

released when a court heard of his hard life as an MP. You may not get away with murder, but it seems being an MP helps you get away with shop-lifting. Fergus went on to become "Sir Fergus" and an important MP. So that's all right ... unless you're the bookseller of course!

6 John Stonehouse. Criminals go to jail and sew mailbags. Politicians like John Stonehouse became Postmaster General (1966–1970) and *bought* the mailbags. But John Stonehouse made a lot of money from cheating business deals. When detectives began investigating John, it looked like he was going to end up sewing those bags – in prison! So he went across to Miami, left his clothes on the beach and disappeared. "Poor man. Walked into the sea and drowned himself," they said. Then he was spotted a couple of months later, in Australia. He wasn't drowned – he wasn't even wet. And, no, he hadn't swum from Miami to Australia. He'd faked his death. You may be pleased to know he ended up sewing mailbags.

7 Graham Riddick. MPs ask questions in Parliament. That's their job. Often those questions (and the answers) help people in business. In fact people in business can make a lot of money if the right questions are asked. So, why don't they offer MPs, say, £1,000 to ask a question? Why not? Because it isn't fair – the rich bribe MPs and get richer while the poor stay poor. So what should Graham Riddick have said when someone phoned and asked him to ask a question for £1,000? He *should* have said "No." What did he say? He said, "Yes." Unfortunately the offer was a trick, set up by

The Sunday Times newspaper. Graham Riddick gave up his job as a government minister ... but he stayed on as an MP and 156 Conservative MPs wrote a letter supporting him! (Although the Prime Minister at the time, John Major, set up a committee to investigate the allegations.) An average MP asks 90 questions a year. Imagine getting £1,000 every time you asked one! Cash for questions has since been banned.

8 Horatio Bottomley became an MP in 1908 and stayed in Parliament for another 14 years even though he was a crook. Usually he promised to make you some money ... if you gave him a lot of money to start with. Mostly he spent your money on himself; he was very fond of champagne. He was charged several times but always managed to talk his way out of it, until 1922 when he met a very tough judge.

The judge said, "I sentence you to seven years' hard labour for your despicable crime. Take him away."

Bottomley objected, "I thought a judge was supposed to ask if I had anything to say!"

"Not in a fraud case," the judge snapped.

Bottomley shrugged. "I just wanted to tell you that I think you did an awful job on my case."

This bit of cheek did not do him any good. His champagne life was over. So were his days as an MP.

Quick quote: "Any fool can tell the truth. But it takes a man of some sense to tell a lie well." (R A Butler, Conservative minister 1940s, 50s and 60s.)

Potty political fact: The Whips are watching you

Don't think it is only the newspaper reporters or the Opposition parties who are watching your behaviour as an MP. Your *own* party is watching you too! The Whips don't just make sure you vote in the right way at the right time. They also keep a Black Book with notes about your dodgy friends and some of the stories that are passed around about you ... even if the stories are untrue!

JUST LIKE SCHOOL RECORD CARDS IN FACT!

Potty politician

Everyone knows that the first woman to be elected to the British Parliament was Lady Astor in 1921.

Everyone is *wrong!* The first woman to be elected was one of the sixteen who stood in 1918. Her name was Constance Georgina, Lady Markievicz. (Try getting that name on your pamphlets! There'd be no room left for her policy!)

Lady M was an Irish Republican who wanted freedom for Ireland. In fact she had been sentenced to death in 1916 for her freedom fighting activities, but had been released.

One of her more daring attacks was on a gentleman's club in Dublin. She left a certain Mr Scovell absolutely furious and demanding an apology.

April, 1916

Dear Gore-Booth,

I really must protest most strongly at the activities of your daughter, Constance Georgina. She has just shot me, and in my club too.

I was having a quiet drink when those Republican johnnies started marching down the street, shouting and letting off bullets. Damned dangerous and it ought to be stopped if you ask me. Anyway, one of these damned bullets flies through the window, hits me in the arm and makes me spill my whisky don't you know!

I look up and who do I see, smoking rifle in hand? Your daughter, Constance Georgina. If you can't keep the young woman under proper control then I suggest you keep her in the house under lock and key before the police do.

The arm will mend and it's no use crying over spilt whisky, but as one gentleman to another, Gore-Booth, I insist on an apology.

Arthur Scovell

Scovell probably got his apology; Lady M certainly was arrested. When the 1918 elections came around she stood for Parliament and was elected. Constance Georgina believed that Ireland should be ruled by an Irish Parliament so she refused to take her seat in the Westminster Parliament.

There were probably 706 very relieved men in Westminster when they heard she (and her rifle) were staying in Dublin!

BATTY BUDGETS

The Government spends a lot of money. It has to pay MPs' wages, roads for our cars to run on, MPs' wages, Armed Forces and their weapons to defend us, MPs' wages, schools and teachers, MPs' wages, hospitals, medicines, nurses and doctors, payments to the unemployed and, of course, MPs' wages.

It gets most of the money it needs from taxes. Taxes like ...

- Income tax ... the Government takes 22p every time you earn £1. (When this tax was first invented it was just 2.5p.)
- Value added tax (VAT) ... a tax on things you buy (like televisions, computers, and paper clips) and services you buy (like having those televisions and computers fixed when they blow up ... or paperclips bent back when they get straightened).
- National Insurance ... people who work pay this so they get free care from doctors and hospitals (except it isn't free because they pay National Insurance AND they pay for medicines!).
- Road fund tax ... paid for that little tax disc stuck in the corner of every car's windscreen.

The Government has to try and spend just what it gets in taxes – no more – like you and your pocket money. This is the Government's "Budget".

But in the last 20 years the biggest problem with money has been something called inflation ... where prices go up and up and up.

You know the sort of thing; your granny says ...

If you are going to be a politician you have to be able to answer the question ... if you're going to be a politician you have to be able to answer questions like, "What are you going to do about inflation?" You could start by teaching it in schools. How about inflated stories like this one. Take one off each number to make sense ...

GOLDILOCKS

TWICE upon a time there were four bears. The bears always nine porridge for breakfast. Two day they decided to pick three-lips in the five-rest be-five they sat down and nine. Baby Bear said, "Three-dle-oo, little house" and put his three yards on the floor.

They stayed out three long because they were separ-nined in the forest. By the time they returned at thirteen o'clock a little girl called Goldilocks had scoffed all their porridge. The three faced little girl blamed Baby Bear.

"I get the blame five everything." Baby Bear cried as Daddy Bear gave him seven of the best on his eleven-der behind, "I'm as seven as a parrot!" He got bread without water even though he was secondy.

Goldilocks ran off laughing, licking her three-lips and Baby Bear never five-gave her, not even when he was very, very dead. The End.

Potty political fact: Painful times

18th century Prime Minister William Pitt once put a tax on windows. The more windows in your house

108

the more tax you paid. Many meanies had their windows bricked up to save money!

Budget bullying

Lloyd George was known as the Welsh Wizard because he was so crafty (and because he was Welsh, of course). In 1909 he promised to tax the rich to give to the poor ... a bit like Robin Hood with the law on his side. There are more poor than rich and they all voted for this great idea.

Of course the Lords in the House of Lords objected. They would do ... they were the rich, weren't they?

They threatened to scrap this tax idea ... so the Liberals threatened to make so many new Liberal Lords that the House of Lords would be full of Liberals and the law would be passed anyway. This bullying worked. The Lords passed the new taxes and promised never to object to money laws ever again.

Ninety years later they are still keeping to that promise. *That's* what you call bullying.

Top tips 7: Save and spend

If you are the Prime Minister then *cut* taxes and *spend* loads of money just before an election. People will think this is great and vote for you. After you have been voted back as Prime Minister you can put taxes back up and cut the spending you promised.

Every government does this ... and the people very often fall for it.

Quick quote: "I am proud to be paying taxes in the United States. The only thing is ... I could be just as proud for half the amount of money." (Comedian Arthur Godfrey.)

POTTY PRIME MINISTERS

The top job in British politics is Prime Minister. The leader of the party that wins a General Election becomes Prime Minister. Of course, the Prime Minister has to answer all the hard questions, but has a gang of ministers and secretaries to help.

If most MPs are good at dodging questions then the Prime Minister has to be a real expert!

> **Quick quote:** "I must follow the people for I am their leader." (Prime Minister Benjamin Disraeli.)

Peculiar premiers

It's a bit worrying when you think about it. All that power in the hands of one person – the Prime Minister. Especially when you look at some of the peculiar Prime Ministers we've had in Britain. Bullies, cowards, drunkards, drug addicts and wimps – not to mention a few potty ones. Britain has had them all …

1 William Pitt (the elder), The Earl of Chatham, 1708–1778. An honest politician who refused to make money from his government jobs. (The strain of trying to stay honest was tremendous … be warned!) He became so depressed he was considered insane.

HE'S A PITT OF DESPAIR

The treatment at that time was to lock him in a darkened room. His wife passed food to him through a hatch. He continued to work until it killed him. He collapsed while making a speech in the House of Lords.

2 Lord North, 1732–1792. His Lordship did not take his job as Prime Minister too seriously. He has been called the worst Prime Minister ever. One day in Parliament Lord Greville made a speech about the history of British taxes. Lord North was bored. He turned to his neighbour and said, "Wake me up when he gets to modern times." He then nodded off to sleep. Half an hour later his neighbour prodded him, North woke and listened to the speech for a few minutes. He turned angrily to the man who'd prodded him. "Zounds!" he cursed. "You've wakened me a hundred years too soon!"

3 Horace Walpole, 1717–1797. Horace was a powerful Prime Minister, but the king, George II, used him as a messenger boy at times. George once sent Walpole to buy a bunch of lottery tickets for one of his girlfriends! (Lottery tickets were also useful gifts to give to people as bribes in the 18th century.) Imagine Queen Elizabeth II sending Tony Blair to the post box to send off her Football Pools!

4 Henry Addington, 1759–1844. Addington was one of the many Prime Ministers who suffered from drink or drug problems. He hadn't the nerve to speak in the Commons till he had drunk at least four bottles of wine.

George Canning was Prime Minister in 1827 and his problem was taking a drug called laudanum. This not only helped him to govern the country – it also helped him to govern his girlfriend, Caroline, who just happened to be the Princess of Wales. Lord Melbourne was full of drink *and* drugs during Queen Victoria's coronation in 1837 while Herbert Asquith (Prime Minister 1908–1916) once sat down in Parliament too drunk to speak.

5 William Pitt (the younger), 1759–1806. Like his dad he was an honest politician. Incredibly he became the youngest British Prime Minister ever when he was 24. He then went on to break another record that he wasn't so pleased with. He became the youngest to *die* when he was just 46. The strain of 19 years as Prime Minister may have helped to kill him – the large amounts of port that he drank almost certainly did.

6 The Duke of Portland, 1738–1809. Portland had been Prime Minister in 1783. When Pitt died the king, George III, appointed Portland again. But by then the wrinklie Portland was practically senile. The Cabinet Ministers held meetings – they didn't bother inviting old Portland and didn't usually tell him what was happening.

7 Spencer Perceval, 1762–1812. Another record-breaker, but he wasn't celebrating. The only British Prime Minister to be assassinated! A madman, Henry Bellingham, got it into his head that Perceval was to blame for all his money problems. He walked into the House of Commons and shot the Prime Minister. Bellingham was tried and executed within a week – very nearly another record! Heartbroken mobs in the Midlands ran through the streets shouting, "Perceval is dead! Hurrah!" Not a popular little Perceval.

8 The Duke of Wellington, 1769–1852. Wellington was a tough old boot. He'd beaten Napoleon and the French at the Battle of Waterloo. (That's Waterloo

113

village in Belgium, not Waterloo Station in London.) When he became Prime Minister in 1828 he was not going to put up with people insulting him. When Lord Winchelsea claimed that Wellington was a Catholic supporter (a great insult in 1829), Wellington challenged him to a duel. Wellington fired first – he aimed at Winchelsea's legs because he wanted to teach the man a lesson, not kill him. The man who had defeated the French was actually a rotten shot – he missed! Winchelsea fired in the air and apologized. Winchelsea got his revenge later by defeating Wellington in a Parliamentary vote.

9 Benjamin Disraeli, 1804–1881. Queen Victoria's favourite Prime Minister because he was a bit of a royal creep. His greatest enemy for many years was William Gladstone. Disraeli began as Conservative Chancellor but Gladstone made a brilliant speech for the Liberals and defeated him in Parliament. Gladstone took over as Chancellor and asked for the Chancellor's robes. Disraeli, like a spoilt child, refused to hand them over. There is a story that someone asked Disraeli the difference between a "misfortune" and a "calamity." He replied, "If Mr Gladstone fell in the Thames it would be a misfortune; but if someone pulled him out it would be a calamity."

10 Lord Salisbury, 1830–1903. Lord Salisbury was too scared of bullies to go to school … when he was an adult! When he went to Eton as a boy he wrote home, "I am bullied from morning till night. I am forced to hide myself in some corner all evening. When I go in to dinner they kick me and I am forced to go out of dinner without eating anything". Would you send your children to this awful school? Lord

Salisbury did! The trouble was he was afraid to take his two sons and sent them off with his wife to Eton.

Top tips 8: Money for nothing?

Get yourself elected Prime Minister as soon as you can. If you are a really good girl (like Margaret Thatcher) you can do it.

ON THE OTHER HAND, LLOYD GEORGE BECAME PRIME MINISTER EVEN THOUGH HE WAS A VERY NAUGHTY BOY!

The Prime Minister is entitled to £143,860 (although Tony Blair receives only £105,233, having stated on 8 May 1997 that the Prime Minister and Cabinet Ministers would not take their post-election pay increases). He gets two houses (10 Downing Street in London and a mansion called Chequers in the country) and is driven around in a posh car.

An ordinary MP gets a basic salary of just £45,066 although the MP also receives a maximum of £12,717 to cover the cost of staying in London and £49,232 to pay office and secretarial costs. They also have to travel backwards and forwards to the town that elected them so they can listen to the voters' problems. (Even if the voter didn't vote for them!) If you can't be Prime Minister then be one of the other ministers. Not only are they well paid but they also get lots of goodies like trips to faraway places. If they say they need their husband/wife with them then the Government pays for the husband/wife to go too! Conservative minister Michael Heseltine took his wife to Australia and South Africa in 1994 and it cost taxpayers (that's you and me) £19,910!

Quick quote: "Here comes the Westminster Ripper." (Labour MP Dennis Skinner talking about Conservative Prime Minister Margaret Thatcher.)

Potty political fact:

Did you know that a Prime Minister may live in 10 Downing Street but is never given the key of the door ... there's always a servant or a policeman to open it for him or her?

AND WHAT TIME DO YOU CALL THIS? I'VE BEEN WORRIED SICK! YOU DIDN'T PHONE, YOU DIDN'T...

And the street is named after Mr Downing ... a man described by 17th-century writers as a "rogue" and a "traitor" who worked for Oliver Cromwell's Parliament then switched sides to support Charles II when the monarchy returned.

He was a greedy, treacherous creep ... in fact Mr Downing sounds like a perfect man to name a Prime Minister's home after!

LOONY LORDS

Of course, if you are a great success as a politician then you can retire and join the House of Lords. Ex-Prime Ministers end up there anyway.

There are other ways to get there of course ...
- be a royal prince (1 out of 1,290)
- be an Archbishop or Bishop (26)
- be a Lord (1,133)
- be a Lady (103)
- be a senior judge (27)

Potty political fact: The best seats in the House

The best seats in the House of Lords are for the bishops. They are the only ones with arm rests – they were put there to stop the bishops falling off when they were drunk (and perhaps still are there for that!).

Top tips 9:

It helps to be a Conservative if you want a place in the House of Lords. There were 474 Conservatives there in 1997 – nearly three times as many as Labour supporters.

Mappin the moggy murderer

Most people think that new laws are thought up by MPs, then go to the House of Lords to be altered. But that's not the whole story. In fact new laws can start in the House of Lords and then go to the Commons.

In the 1930s an article appeared in London evening newspapers that shocked some people. It concerned plans by Sir Charles Mappin of the House of Lords ...

The Evening News April 1, 1937
Stray Cat Clearance Scheme

London's stray cats may not be a problem for much longer. They are to be hunted down if a new scheme becomes law. Sir Charles Mappin today announced a new bill which he plans to put before the House of Lords next week. "My bill will allow packs of greyhounds to hunt cats through the streets of London the way hounds destroy foxes in the countryside." Sir Charles said, "This will have a double advantage; it will introduce a new activity for sporting men and women in the capital and it will also rid the city of vermin. The packs of hounds would earn their keep because the skins of the cats can be sold to the fur trade – so long as the hounds don't

---

rip them too badly, of course. Fox hunters wear those glorious pink jackets; the cat hunters will wear yellow and the sight of them following the hounds on horseback will be a great tourist attraction!" he added.

A spokesman for the Royal Society for the Protection of Cruelty to Animals said, "The RSPCA will almost certainly oppose this law when it is put before the House of Commons. If stray cats are becoming a nuisance then there are kinder ways to dispose of them."

A London County Council Sanitary Inspector said, "Stray cats are unhygienic. On the other hand they do keep the rat population down. We haven't had an outbreak of bubonic plague in London for a long time. We will take a serious look at this proposal."

"It's a great idea" say rats.

Sir Charles says there are at least a hundred members of the Lords keen to try the new sport. "Some have already put in orders for yellow riding coats."

London cat owners are being advised to make sure their pets wear collars with clear name tags. "We wouldn't want the greyhounds to shred a tame tabby by mistake," he said.

If there are no objections in Parliament the Cat Hunting Bill could be law by summer in time for the first packs to begin killing on 1 November, the traditional start of the fox hunting season.

HERE KITTY KITTY!

Sir Charles: Mad Catter.

A lot of very angry letters went to the newspapers, to MPs and to Sir Charles himself. The RSPCA began to plan a campaign to save the cats and London police said they were very concerned about traffic problems caused by hunters and hounds charging through the streets of London.

At that point Sir Charles Mappin came clean. He admitted it was all a great joke dreamed up by some bored lords!

This is a great pity. It is one of the few really good ideas the House of Lords has ever had!

Potty political fact: Lords above!

Lords comment on laws that common people must obey. But lords don't always understand the "common" life.

Lord Curzon usually took a private car or a taxi when he visited London in the 1920s. One day he decided to take a bus, just to see how the ordinary people got about. He complained bitterly, "These bus things aren't as good as they are supposed to be. I caught one at Whitehall and told the driver to take me to Carlton House Terrace. But the driver chap simply refused!"

MAD MONARCHY

Britain is a "monarchy" because the official head is a "monarch". But countries don't have to have a monarch these days if they don't want to. Countries like France, Germany, the USA and Eire don't have a monarch. They vote to have a President instead.

Britain's Parliament could vote to get rid of the Queen tomorrow if it really wanted to. It could vote to replace the Queen with a President ... or even a new queen (or king).

Quick quote: "What are we going to do about the Royal Family? They are so stupid!" (Margaret Thatcher, Prime Minister 1979–90.)

If you are Prime Minister you are at the top of the tree. There is no higher for you to go ... unless you decided to make yourself queen. But would you want to? Being queen has its problems!

EPILOGUE

The Greeks thought everyone should have a say in how their lives are run. Great idea. They called it "democracy".

But what happens if *half* the people want one thing and the *other* half want something else? Have a vote. Everyone must agree that the winner gets to choose.

You can do it in your school. Ask a hundred pupils, "Do you want school uniform?"

Have a vote. The answer may be …

Yes – 51

No – 45

Did not vote – 4 (there are always some!)

So, everyone wears school uniform! That's democracy!

Er ... unfortunately life isn't as simple as that. Suppose you have five choices?

Do you want school uniform for ...
a) Everyone
b) No one
c) All girls
d) Everyone under 14
e) Everyone over 14

Now, suppose the result of a hundred votes is ...
a) 25
b) 20
c) 15
d) 20
e) 15
Did not vote – 5

a) Wins with 25 votes. So *everyone* wears school uniform ... but only 25 people voted for it. 70 people voted AGAINST it and five didn't vote or didn't care.

25 people have decided what 100 people are going to do. Potty!

WHO VOTED FOR THIS ?!!

Parliament in the United Kingdom is a bit like that. In the 1997 election 31.5 million voted. The result was...

Conservatives	9.6 million
Labour	13.5 million
Liberal-Democrat	5.2 million
Others	2.8 million.

Labour won ... but only 13.5 million voted *for* them and 18 million voted *against* them.

This is seriously potty.

In the 1992 elections, one man decided to enter with his own party. He had a great idea. He wanted to tell everyone his "Big Idea" and it was this:

That way the system would collapse and a new, better system would have to be invented. He pleaded, "Don't vote for the Conservatives or the Labour Party or the Liberals." What happened? 121 people voted for him! 121 people did not understand his simple message! It makes you wonder: how many of the other 32 million who voted that year knew what they were really voting for?

Hopefully, when you get the vote, you will realize just how potty politics really is.

So why doesn't somebody do something about it? Winston Churchill probably summed it up when he said ...

Quick quote: "Democracy is the worst system ... except for all the others."

And Winston saw some of "the others" in action. He saw Adolf Hitler's dictatorship in Germany and he saw Joseph Stalin's communism in Russia – they were just as potty as Britain's democracy but they were a hundred times more cruel and unfair.

At least you can laugh at the daft MPs and the crazy system. People who laughed at Mr Hitler or Mr Stalin sometimes never laughed again.

So, until you come up with something better – something less potty – then Britain is stuck with its potty politics. Enjoy it!

LINWOOD HIGH SCHOOL LIBRARY